Uprooting Rejection

Replacing the Root of Rejection with the
Unconditional Love of God!
Ephesians 3:17

Preface

As we were continuing to work on chapters for our upcoming *Mirror Mirror* book which will include messages of all the past years of Mirror Mirror and Kingdom Fest Conferences, I began to realize that the individual messages could not wait until the entire book was completed. I decided to release smaller books, each covering one of the messages. To date, the smaller books include *Power, Love and a Sound Mind*, *Determined* (mini-book), and, now, *Uprooting Rejection*. After the release of all of the smaller books, they will be compiled into the *Mirror Mirror* book.

I would like to thank dear friend and ministry partner, Stephanie Zulauf, for her tremendous help with this book. Her attention to detail and untiring efforts speak volumes. I could not have completed this book without her.

Table of Contents

Third Edition: December 2019

Introduction

As in our first book, *Power, Love and a Sound Mind*, we opened with what we called a *starter prayer*. We would like to continue with that tradition. This is a simple prayer to help you get your eyes off of what you are struggling with and onto the living God. So, here we go:

Heavenly Father, You are the Great I AM and I worship You. Heavenly Father, you know how the actions and words of others have negatively affected me. Please help me to remember that their actions toward me are not Your actions. Their words about me are not Your words. Their thoughts concerning me are not Your thoughts. Help me to replace the memories of hurt in my mind with Your actions, Your words and Your thoughts. Help me to replace the memories of hurt in my heart with Your sweet and unconditional love, grace, and mercy. Help me to see myself through Your eyes, the eyes of my loving Heavenly Father. Help me to forgive those who have rejected and hurt me. And, if I have hurt or wronged another, please forgive me. I am truly sorry. All glory and praise to You, Lord. I pray this in the name of my Savior, Jesus Christ. Amen

Throughout the book you will see references to "Reflections". These "Reflections", located in the back of the book, are written to help guide you through your healing journey. I strongly encourage you to take the time to complete these "Reflections". Your understanding and appreciation of God's life-changing, unconditional love will be greatly increased as a result.

Chapter 1 - Uprooting Rejection

In preparing for this book, I began to reminisce about the many stories that others have told me, as well as my own memories, of the sting of rejection. From the girl who told us she was called fat and ugly all of her life, to the one who was told he/she just *didn't have what it takes* to make it in this world, we can all relate to the pain and loneliness caused by being rejected.

I remember the pangs of feeling rejected in different ways in my early middle school years. It wasn't until years later that I realized that *that* desire to be accepted (and not rejected), led me to become very *performance and works* driven, not only in life but also in my early years of Christianity. My identity had become terribly wrapped up with all of the *things* I was doing for the Lord.

As I look back, I realize that these things were simply the result of not knowing the unconditional love of our Heavenly Father. I didn't realize that Our God loves us unconditionally, regardless of what or how much we do for Him! I remember thinking that I had to somehow *earn brownie points* to maintain my position with God; that the more *works* I did for him, the more secure I would be. It wasn't until I literally broke under the weight of such nonsense that I learned that nothing could be further from the truth. God was not and is not interested in *how much* I can do for Him! He simply wants me to be His daughter; one He loves unconditionally, one for whom He died and has an incredible plan! (I go into further detail of this in my book, *Power, Love and a Sound Mind.*) The same is true for you!

The more I began to understand the truth of God's unconditional love for me, the more I began to experience and enjoy the freedoms that come simply from being a *child of God*.

But, as I have been able to continue in my journey, free and unhindered from any past feelings of rejection, I have noticed that others have not been so fortunate. As a minister communicating with people from all walks of life, I have seen the lasting negative effects of rejection.

As I shared in the very beginning of this chapter, some of their stories have been devastating. Their experiences with rejection have left them with, not only suffering in silence, but also of not knowing how to walk away from those wounds and hurts and into the freedoms that Christ died to give us!

The Effects of Rejection

Some forms of rejection can be brushed off of your shoulder like a piece of lint, while others, unless dealt with, can hang onto a person for an entire lifetime. That person has no idea that he/she is viewing life from *a lens of being rejected*, causing all types of troubled behavior and living life perhaps much differently than ever intended.

The pangs of rejection can have detrimental and long lasting effects.

I cannot imagine someone *not* having gone through the pains of rejection at some time in his or her life! Rejection is a part of the fallen world in which we live. There is no escaping it!

Even Jesus did not escape rejection. From the beginning of his ministry, people doubted who He was and questioned His authenticity and His words.

> *Is this not the carpenter, the Son of Mary,*
> *and brother of James, Joses, Judas, and*
> *Simon? And are not His sisters here with*
> *us?" So they were offended at Him.*
> Mark 6:3 (NKJV)

> *For even His brothers did not believe in Him.*
> John 7:5 (NKJV)

> *He was despised and forsaken of men,*
> *A man of sorrows and acquainted with grief;*
> *And like one from whom men hide their face*
> *He was despised, and we did not esteem*
> *Him.*
> Isaiah 53:3 (NKJV)

Rejection has many faces, but the pain that results is universal.

It is imperative that we know:
- the truths with regard to what rejection is
- how rejection may have transpired in our lives
- what *God* has to say about rejection
- how to replace rejection with the unconditional love of God

>> See <u>Reflection #1</u> in the back of the book. <<

Chapter 2 - The Truths with Regard to What Rejection Is

It's interesting to note that in his book, *The Search for Significance*, author Robert McGee says that rejection is actually a type of communication. It *says* something. Robert McGee states: "It conveys a message that someone is unsatisfactory to us, that he or she doesn't measure up to a standard we've created or adopted."[1]

Rejection means being told - I don't want you. You have no value. "Usually rejection is manifested by an outburst of anger, a disgusted look, an impatient answer, or a social snub. Whatever the form of behavior, it communicates disrespect, low value, and a lack of appreciation. Nothing hurts quite like the message of rejection." [2]

In order to receive healing in any area of hurt, and in this case, with the hurt of rejection, we need to understand the origin of that hurt.

Where did rejection begin?

Then God said, "Let Us make man in Our image, according to Our likeness; let them

*have dominion over the fish of the sea, over
the birds of the air, and over the cattle, over
all the earth and over every creeping thing
that creeps on the earth." So God created
man **in His own image; in the image of God**
He created him; male and female He created
them. Then God blessed them, and God said
to them, "Be fruitful and multiply; fill the
earth and subdue it; have dominion over the
fish of the sea, over the birds of the air, and
over every living thing that moves on the
earth."*
Genesis 1:26-28 (NKJV)
[Bold added for emphasis]

*Then God saw everything that He had made,
and indeed **it was very good**.*
Genesis 1:31 (NKJV)
[Bold added for emphasis]

*The Lord God planted a garden eastward in
Eden, and there He put the man whom He
had formed.*
Genesis 2:8 (NKJV)

*Then the Lord God took the man and put him
in the garden of Eden to tend and keep it.
And the Lord God commanded the man,
saying, "Of every tree of the garden you may
freely eat; but of the tree of the knowledge of*

good and evil you shall not eat, for in the day
that you eat of it you shall surely die."
Genesis 2:15-17 (NKJV)

And the Lord God caused a deep sleep to fall
on Adam, and he slept; and He took one of
his ribs, and closed up the flesh in its place.
Then the rib which the Lord God had taken
from man He made into a woman, and He
brought her to the man.
Genesis 2:21-22 (NKJV)

The reason I bring up the beginnings of man in the book of Genesis is I want you to see that i*n the beginning* there was no such thing as *rejection,* shame, fear of man, anger, bitterness, or any such negative emotions! Notice **Genesis 1:31.** Then God saw everything that He had made, and indeed "**it was very good.**"

It isn't until **Genesis Chapter 3**, with the *origin of man's sin,* where we see things begin to crumble. You may know the story well, but I will include it here so that you can see where rejection has its origin.

*Now the **serpent** was more cunning than any*
beast of the field which the Lord God had
made. And he said to the woman, "Has God
indeed said, 'You shall not eat of every tree
of the garden'?"
And the woman said to the serpent, "We may
eat the fruit of the trees of the garden; but of

the fruit of the tree which is in the midst of
the garden, God has said, 'You shall not eat
it, nor shall you touch it, lest you die.' "
Then the serpent said to the woman, "You
will not surely die.

Genesis 3:1-4 (NKJV)
[Bold added for emphasis]

The serpent was very deceptive. God said that Adam and Eve would die and He meant what He said! But, as you already most likely know, Adam and Eve did not heed God's warning. They disobeyed. They ate of the fruit, and as a result, they did, indeed die.

The word *die* here does not mean *die* as in *cease to live* because we know that Adam and Eve continued to live physically. But the word *die* here means *to die spiritually*; to be separated from God. What a tragedy! No more innocence. No more "walking with God in the garden in the cool of the day." (Genesis 3:8). Adam and Eve were stripped of that beautiful pure communication with God. They had sinned and they were the cause.

Adam and Eve put their self (selfish) desires (eating the fruit) above the desire of God (not eating the fruit) (Genesis 3:6). This active and selfish disobedience was the origin of sin. Here, at the very first appearance of *self* and, therefore, sin, we see, that instead of the beautiful ability to communicate with God and enjoy Him, things turned inward and *self* began to demand its way. What was once the most amazing awareness of God, (God-consciousness), suddenly turned into the destructive awareness of *self* and what we call *self-consciousness*.

Folks, this is where rejection began! It began here because this is where *self* began! And, the result of anything having to do with *self* is **detrimental fruit**! Rather than the simple purity and innocence of knowing the love of God, when *self* appeared, the opposite emotions began to rear their ugly heads - among them: doubt, anger, and rejection. Everything got turned wrong-side out and upside-down!

>> See <u>Reflection #2</u> in the back of the book. <<

Chapter 3 - How Rejection May Have Transpired in Our Lives

One definition of *rejection* is: the ignoring, overlooking or casting aside of someone or something. Rejection can often start in our lives when we are very young. An example might be someone's words that were spoken to you or about you, and those words crushed you. Another example might be the sting of someone's condescending look or disapproving attitude. Rejection may also take the form of being compared unfavorably to a sibling, being abandoned, someone withholding his/her love or not accepting your love, not being accepted by peers, repeated unfulfillment of promises, or unacceptance because of a physical or learning disability.

These things begin to form an image of yourself *to* yourself, or we may say that these things begin to form your *self-image*. Self image is the mental picture that you have of yourself. That mental picture is planted in the soil of your heart. Not knowing how to "extract the picture", we let it lay there until it begins to "get rooted", growing deeply and strongly in our thoughts and in our hearts.

"A tree is known by its fruit."

*For a good tree does not bear bad fruit, nor does a bad tree bear good fruit. **For every tree is known by its own fruit.***
Luke 6:43-44 (NKJV)
[Bold added for emphasis]

As you can see in Luke 6:43-44, **what is rooted in your heart will determine the fruit in your life. This is a most crucial truth!**

The table on the next page lists the detrimental fruit that can result from the root of rejection.

The Root of Rejection Yields the Fruit of Rejection
defensiveness
hardness
anger
rebellion
disrespect
anxiety
depression
insecurities
competition
jealousy
perfectionism
meanness
wishing ill will of others
seeking vengeance
bitterness
inconsistency
impatience
loneliness
fear of what someone thinks about you

>> See Reflection #3 in the back of the book. <<

Chapter 4 - What *God* Has to Say About Rejection

But take heart, precious reader! God has something to say about this thing called rejection and its negative fruit! Just look at these encouraging, life-changing Scriptures! These all speak volumes pertaining to the outstanding, unconditional love that God has just for you! **And, *that*, dear reader, is the solution to suffering from the pangs of rejection — <u>knowing the unconditional love that our Lord has just for you!</u>**

God will not leave you the way he found you!

*A bruised reed **He will not break***
*And a dimly burning wick **He will not extinguish**;*
He will faithfully bring forth justice.
Isaiah 43:3 (NKJV)
[Bold added for emphasis]

*He **restores** my soul;*
He guides me in the paths of righteousness
For His name's sake.
Psalm 23:3 (NKJV)
[Bold added for emphasis]

The word *restore* here means *to turn back* or to bring back to a source of refreshment and health.

He heals the brokenhearted
And binds up their wounds [healing their
pain and comforting their sorrow].
Psalm 147:3 (AMP)
[Bold added for emphasis]

God's Spirit is on me;
he's chosen me to preach the Message of
good news to the poor,
Sent me to announce pardon to prisoners and
recovery of sight to the blind,
To set the burdened and battered free,
to announce, "This is God's year to act!
Luke 4:18-19 (MSG)
[Bold added for emphasis]

Before I formed you in the womb I knew you
[and approved of you as My chosen
instrument],
And before you were born I consecrated you
[to Myself as My own];

I have appointed you as a prophet to the nations.

Jeremiah 1:5 (AMP)
[Bold added for emphasis]

The above scriptures all point to the solution for suffering the pangs of rejection. It is this - **replace rejection with the unconditional love of God**. (I give practical steps on how to go about doing this in the next chapter, beginning with **Healing Begins in the Presence of God**.)

Chapter 5 - The Solution to Overcoming the Root of Rejection: Replace Rejection with the Unconditional Love of God

*...May you be **rooted deep** in love and*
founded securely on love,
Ephesians 3:17 (AMPC)
[Bold added for emphasis]

God chose us in love! Once you realize the astounding love that God has for you - **once you allow His love to be your root system** - just the *opposite* of all of those negative fruit(s) will begin to take root. Your *new* fruit will start to grow! Your *root* system will get cleaned out and filled up with God's unconditional love.

Out with the old. In with the new!

The left hand side of the table lists the detrimental fruit that can result from the root of rejection. See, in the right column of the table, how the fruit changes when we change the root system to that of the **unconditional love of God**.

The Root of Rejection Yields the Fruit of Rejection	The Root of God's Unconditional Love Yields the Fruit of God's Unconditional Love
defensiveness	openness
hardness	gentleness*
anger	self-control*
rebellion	submission
disrespect	respect
anxiety	peace*
depression	joy*
insecurities	confidence
competition	security
jealousy	contentment
perfectionism	security
meanness	kindness*
wishing ill will of others	goodness*
seeking vengeance	forgiveness
bitterness	love*
inconsistency	faithfulness*
impatience	longsuffering*
loneliness	fellowship
fear of what someone thinks about you	trust in what God says about you

* Fruit of the Spirit. Galatians 5:22-23

>> See <u>Reflection #4</u> in the back of the book. <<

You are getting uprooted out of the *old* and getting planted into the *new - into Christ.* We can say it this way, you are becoming rooted in HIM now. Your goal is to get so deeply rooted in Christ, that nothing will be able to uproot you from His love.

I had the opportunity to share this message with an amazing group of women. One of the women who attended was, Women's Pastor and very dear friend, Pastor Parris Bailey. She gave a great illustration of what this also might look like! "Picture you are taking a plant and placing its roots into a waste dump filled with toxic chemicals! There's not much of a chance for that plant to survive, (let alone grow and become beautiful!) But what if you took that plant, (uprooted it) and placed its roots into the richest brown soil and then added the healthiest of nutrients? That plant would soon begin, not only to survive, but, it would begin to grow and thrive and eventually display its beauty. What happened? ***You changed its root system!"***

This is the best news ever! Suffering from a *root of rejection* does not have to be your story any longer! Get overwhelmed with the love of God! **His love is so powerful it will bring complete healing to your mind, body soul, and spirit!**

So how do you do that? **How do you experience the unconditional love of God for yourself?** Maybe you've recognized some of the <u>detrimental</u> fruit in your life. You are now ready to be free! What do you do?

== Healing Begins in the Presence of God ==

You will show me the path of life;
*In Your **presence is fullness of joy**;*
At Your right hand are pleasures
forevermore.
> Psalm 16:11 (NKJV)
> [Bold added for emphasis]

As we see in Psalm 16:11, it is in God's Presence that we will find fullness of joy! **It is in His Presence where we will begin to experience true, unconditional love and acceptance.** *This* atmosphere, *His atmosphere*, will begin to cut through all of those painful memories or current stings of being rejected.

Think about this.

For You formed my inward parts;
You covered me in my mother's womb. I will
praise You, for I am fearfully and
wonderfully made;
Marvelous are Your works,

And that my soul knows very well.
My frame was not hidden from You,
When I was made in secret,
And skillfully wrought in the lowest parts of
the earth.
Your eyes saw my substance, being yet
unformed.
And in Your book they all were written,
The days fashioned for me,
When as yet there were none of them.
How precious also are Your thoughts to me,
O God!
How great is the sum of them!
If I should count them, they would be more
in number than the sand;
When I awake, I am still with You.
Psalm 139:13-18 (NKJV)
[Bold added for emphasis]

According to the University of Hawaii, there are 7 quintillion, 5 quadrillion grains of sand on planet earth. That's the number 75 followed by 17 zeros! [3]

7,500,000,000,000,000,000

This is how many thoughts God has about you! This is not the hyperbole of poetry (hyperbole - exaggerated statements or claims not meant to be taken literally). It is God's Word. It is Truth. God thinks about us infinitely - without limit! God loves you beyond anything you can possibly imagine!

Take time *daily* simply enjoying God! Sometimes you can hear this phrase so many times (take time daily enjoying God), that you race right over it. You might even find yourself saying, "yeah, yeah, I got that"! But do you? Do you actually stop whatever it is you are doing and *intentionally* spend time with our Lord? This is critical! *Nothing* can match your quality time with God! *Nothing!* **Healing begins here!**

Jesus also knew His need to spend time with our Heavenly Father. Throughout His ministry, Jesus intentionally spent time alone with the Father. It was during these times that God provided Him with guidance, comfort, and encouragement. The same is true for us.

Maybe you can rise earlier than everyone else in your household while it is still quiet and open your Bible and a notebook and just begin to write all that is on your heart to our Lord. I do this on a regular basis to this day and I love it!

Or maybe you find solace in your car or when you take a walk. Continue to do those things, but how about when you are doing them, *on purpose*, stop, pause and listen! Stop long enough to get your bearings that *this* is going to be *God time*! You then just open your heart and talk with our Lord about whatever might be on your heart! As you are communicating, take the time to pause and see what He would have you to know. You can put on your favorite worship music during these times and allow God's love to pour all over you! **When you do this, you are** *washing out* that old root system and *filling it up* with the love of God! (Your <u>new</u> root system)

== Prayer, Praise, and Power ==

Prayer is the most powerful ability the believer has access to!

And pray in the Spirit on all occasions with
all kinds of prayers and requests. *With this*
in mind, be alert and always keep on praying
for all the Lord's people.
Ephesians 6:18 (NIV)]
[Bold added for emphasis]

Praying *always with all prayer and*
supplication in the Spirit, and watching
thereunto with all perseverance and
supplication for all saints;
Ephesians 6:18 (KJV)
[Bold added for emphasis]

Rick Renner states that *Proseuche* is the word that Paul uses in Ephesians 6:18 (KJV), when he says, "Praying always with all prayer…" *Proseuche* is a compound of the words *pros* and *euche*. The word *pros* is a preposition that means *toward*, and it can denote *a sense of closeness*. The word *proseuche* tells us that prayer should bring us face to face and into close contact with God. Prayer is more than a mechanical act or a formula to follow; it is a vehicle to bring us to a place whereby we may enjoy *a close, intimate relationship with God.* [4]

I love that! What an immense privilege and joy to be able to talk with God directly! Pour your heart out to Him! This is your time to express all that is going on on the inside of you! There are so many powerful Scriptures to pray with regards to **prayer, (petition), and answered prayer,** but two of my favorites are :

> *Pour out **all** your worries and stress upon him and **leave them there**, for he **always** tenderly cares for you.*
>
> 1 Peter 5:7 (TPT)
> [Bold added for emphasis]

> ***Trust** in the Lord completely, and do not rely on your own opinions. **With all your heart** rely on him to guide you, and **he will lead you in every decision you make. Become intimate with him in whatever you do, and he will lead you wherever you go**.*
>
> Proverbs 3:5-6 (TPT)
> [Bold added for emphasis]

== **Combine prayer with praise!** ==

While in the presence of the Lord, combine prayer with praise. Praise takes our focus off of us and our circumstances and places the focus on to God, His limitless power and ability, and His sovereign Kingdom. Praise releases the abundant power of God in our lives.

The following is just one of many powerful Scriptures with regards to prayer and praise and their powerful effects!

> *But at midnight Paul and Silas were praying and singing hymns to God, and the prisoners were listening to them. Suddenly there was a great earthquake, so that the foundations of the prison were shaken; and immediately all the doors were opened and everyone's chains were loosed.*
> Acts 16:25-26 (NKJV)

Beaten and imprisoned, Paul and Silas respond by singing a hymn of praise - **a song sung directly from the heart to God**. The relationship between their song of praise and their supernatural deliverance through the earthquake cannot be overlooked. Their praise was so supernatural that it opened prison doors! Not only were Paul and Silas delivered, but a man was converted, his household saved, and satanic captivity overthrown in Philippi.[5] (The entire event can be found in Acts 16:16-40.)

Never underestimate the power of prayer and praise. That *root of rejection* will begin to come up and out of you and be gone!

**I will not leave you as orphans [comfortless, desolate, bereaved, forlorn, helpless]*; I will come [back] to you.*
John 14:18 (AMPC)
[Bold added for emphasis]

>> See <u>Reflection #5</u> in the back of the book. <<

== Replace Lies with Truth ==

Another critical thing that I have learned to do that has helped me with, not only uprooting rejection, but uprooting other areas of negativity, is to **replace lies with truth**. Replace what was spoken over you or what you may have wrongly believed about yourself with what God says about you (regardless of what has happened to you)!

I have listed 18 examples of *what God says about you* (compared to any lies that you may have believed about yourself), later in this book in **"God Says You Are…"** But to get you started with how to replace lies with truth, let's look at Ephesians 1:4. Ephesians 1:4 states that we have been *chosen* by God!

*just as **He chose us** in Him before the*
foundation of the world, that we should be
holy and without blame before Him in love,
Ephesians 1:4 (NKJV)
[Bold added for emphasis]

***I chose you** before I formed you in the womb*
Jeremiah 1:5 (HCSB)
[Bold added for emphasis]

Christ "chose us" out of the world to *bring us into Himself*!

So if the lie comes to you that you are rejected, **you can replace the lie with the truth that you have been *chosen* by God.**

Go back. Look at those words that were spoken over you and ***replace them with the truth.*** Find your value from what God says about you. Ask Him about your unique wiring, gifts and talents. (Once again, please see the **"God Says You Are…"** *in the back of this book)*

Don't give those words, those condescending looks, those negative comments from your past so much power. If you see yourself beginning to spiral downward, bring those thoughts to the surface and expose them to the light.

>> See <u>Reflection #6</u> in the back of the book. <<

== **Encourage Yourself in the Lord** ==

As we continue practicing ways to ***uproot rejection***, I think back to the times when I have had to *encourage myself in the Lord*, or, as the mother of a dear friend of mine would say, "I had a fireside chat with myself".

As with David in 1 Samuel 30:6, ***there will be times*** when you will have to encourage yourself in the Lord.

> *And David was greatly distressed; for the*
> *people spake of stoning him, because the*
> *soul of all the people was grieved, every man*
> *for his sons and for his daughters:* ***but David***
> ***encouraged himself in the Lord his God.***
> 1 Samuel 30:6 (KJV)
> [Bold added for emphasis]

This was one of the most difficult times in David's life. After a brutal war, David returned to his camp only to find that it had been burned to the ground and everyone in the camp had been taken captive. Because David was the leader, his own people spoke of stoning him because they were so upset! Can you imagine? The hurt and pains of the people were so deep because their sons and daughters were taken captive, that they wanted nothing to do with David! How did David respond? David was initially in anguish, but, as stated in 1 Samuel 30:6, he encouraged himself in the Lord his God. The entire event can be found in 1 Samuel chapter 30.

The word *encouraged* here is *khaw-zak* (Strongs #2388), and it means 'to fasten upon'. David 'fastened himself upon' the Lord His God.

The NIV says "But David *found strength* in the Lord his God." Moffetts translation says "David *relied* on the eternal, his God, and *took courage*." Knox's translation says that "David *found refuge* in the Lord his God."

There are many ways we can encourage ourselves in the Lord, but one way that David could have done this is to remember all the good that the Lord had already done in his life. David could have remembered such things as he was chosen by God. He didn't choose himself to become King of Israel. God chose him! God sent Samuel to anoint David and Samuel spoke over David's life. Through God's enabling power, David killed a lion and a bear. He defeated Goliath. Saul chased David, but he never got him. David could have reminded himself of these past victories and how God was for him throughout his entire journey.

The same is true for you and for me! God is for us! As we have stated earlier, God chose us. (Ephesians 1:4) He bought us with His blood. (1 Peter 1:18-19) We are joint heirs with Jesus Christ. (Romans 8:17) We have been made kings and priests into our God. (Revelation 5:10) We have the Holy Spirit in us helping us. (John 14:16-18) We have the Name of Jesus and the Word of God! (Matthew 28:18-20; Mark 16:17-18; 1 Thessalonians 2:13-16; 2 Timothy 3:16-17; Hebrews 4:12) God will never leave us nor forsake us! (Romans 8:31) We are more than conquerors in Christ! (Romans 8:37) There are so many things we need to be reminded of as we *encourage ourselves in the Lord*!

In dealing with women in so many of my meetings and conferences, one area in particular that I see where women need to encourage themselves in the Lord is when they compare themselves with others. This might seem trivial when compared with something as dire as what David faced, but please remember - we are uprooting rejection. **One sure way to remain in that rejection is to compare yourself to someone else.** Scripture tells us NOT to do this! (Galatians 6:4; 2 Corinthians 10:12) It is SO damaging!

Encourage yourself in the Lord if you are being tempted to compare yourself with someone else, knowing that God has something unique and particular just for YOU! Continue to get established (rooted) in God's unconditional love and His amazing plan carved out from before time began for YOU. Go over all of the powerful truths listed in the **"God Says You Are..."** listed in the back of this book!

Please note that I have a teaching on *The Dangers of Comparison* on my website downloadable for FREE. (ANNADONAHUEMINISTRIES.COM **Free Downloadable Notes**). It was written and shared by my daughter at a recent Kingdom Fest Conference. I think it will benefit you greatly!

>> See <u>Reflection #7</u> in the back of the book. <<

== Forgive ==

As we begin to close out our powerful suggestions of how to uproot rejection and replace it with the unconditional love of God, we include the privileges of receiving forgiveness and forgiving those who have hurt us.

I use the word "privileges" on purpose. It is a privilege to be able to receive forgiveness first and foremost from our Heavenly Father and then to be able to extend forgiveness to those who may have hurt you.

We are all in need of forgiveness!

for all have sinned and fall short of the glory
of God
Romans 3:23 (NKJV)

The amazing thing is, God is **always** ready and willing to forgive us!

But if we freely admit our sins when his light
*uncovers them, **he will be faithful to forgive***
***us every time**. God is just to forgive us our*
sins because of Christ, and he will continue
to cleanse us from all unrighteousness.
1 John 1:9 (TPT)
[Bold added for emphasis]

And isn't it also a tremendous blessing when you have done something that has hurt someone, (knowingly or perhaps unknowingly) and upon becoming aware that you have hurt that person, you ask for forgiveness and the person graciously forgives you. What a joy and relief you receive!

Unforgiveness is a poison. It keeps you bound up in bitterness and torment. Forgiveness however, (both receiving and giving) is beautiful! It allows you to walk in freedom unhindered by hurt and bitterness!

We see that **Jesus commands us to forgive** in Mark 11:25.

> *And when you stand praying, if you hold*
> *anything against anyone, **forgive them**, so*
> *that your Father in heaven may forgive you*
> *your sins.*
>
> Mark 11:25 (NIV)
> [Bold added for emphasis]

And, again in Ephesians 4:32.

> *Be kind and helpful to one another, tender-*
> *hearted [compassionate, understanding],*
> ***forgiving one another** [readily and freely],*
> *just as God in Christ also forgave you.*
>
> Ephesians 4:32 (AMP)
> [Bold added for emphasis]

Forgiveness isn't something that you do just when you feel like it. It isn't simply an emotion. Rather it is an act of your will. If you are thinking that you could never forgive what may have been done to you, please remember, you are not doing this alone! Jesus would never command us to forgive (or to do anything else written in the Bible), if He didn't first give us the ability to do so! We have the power of the Holy Spirit living on the inside of us to do this! If Jesus is commanding us to forgive, then that means that it is possible; not in our own strength, but in His! We make the choice to line up our wills (forgive) with His will. Once that happens, God comes on the scene!

Forgiveness is no small matter! Your very fellowship with God is at stake!

For if you forgive others their trespasses
[their reckless and willful sins], your
*heavenly Father will also forgive you. **But if***
***you do not forgive others** [nurturing your*
hurt and anger with the result that it
interferes with your relationship with God],
then your Father will not forgive your
trespasses.
Matthew 6:14-15 (AMP)
[Bold added for emphasis]

This is your time! This is your day to get free and stay free! Forgiveness is wonderful! Again - it's a privilege! Turn that thing over to God. Give it to Him and let Him heal you! Right now, even as you are reading this, simply bow your head and your heart, and say:

Heavenly Father, I want to obey Your command to forgive those who have hurt me. I know, because You have commanded me to forgive, You will also give me the ability to do so. I need Your help. I give this unforgiveness to You. I give You all of the pain, the memories and the thoughts. I no longer want to hold a grudge. Please help me. Please take this pain of unforgiveness from me as I give it to You. I want to be free. You forgave me. I now choose to forgive _(fill in persons's name or event)_ . Please bring to my attention anyone from whom *I* need to ask *their* forgiveness and give me the courage to do so. Thank You, Lord. I love You! I pray this in Jesus' Name! Amen!

God will take it, my friend! He will then give you the ability to forgive others.

>> See <u>Reflection #8</u> in the back of the book. <<

== **God Can Turn it Around! Let Him!** ==

In my many years of ministry, I have seen so many people find freedom and healing from the hurt of rejection when they allow that hurt to be replaced with the unconditional love of God. Prayerfully, some of these other suggestions that I have listed will be of help to you, as well!

God loves you. God has a plan for your life - a great plan! (Jeremiah 1:5; Jeremiah 29:11; Ephesians 2:10) Whatever has caused rejection in your life, place it on the altar and watch God make use of it! He will turn it around for your good! There is no promise that you will never get hurt again, **but this Scripture promises that <u>God will make it right</u> if you place your trust in Him.**

*And we know that God causes all things to
work together for good to those who love
God, to those who are called according to
His purpose.*
Romans 8:28 (NASB)

Closing Remarks

As with many things in our lives in which we would like to see change, there *is* a requirement that comes from us. We must put in the needed time and energy that it takes in order to *see the change* that we would like to see.

Don't get me wrong. *God* is the One Who does the changing! But, we have our part to play. Uprooting things such as rejection or any other area that we are unhappy with will require that we spend ample amounts of time with God, addressing the issues, discovering the *hows*, the *whys* and the *whens*, but also, rising up and declaring, "Ok. I get it. I will now address those areas with the powerful truths from the Word of God and His amazing love!"

I strongly encourage you to invest the time needed for your healing! I have listed many ways for you to do so. Don't be concerned with how long the process may take. Keep your eyes fixed on Jesus, the "Author and Finisher of your faith" (Hebrews 12:2) and all of the amazing changes you are beginning to see happen on the inside of you! It gets quite exciting actually!

You are changing things in your life that will take you into eternity! And the legacy that you will leave behind? Unparalleled! You will have broken the cycle of *being rejected* and living under its detrimental fruit. Rather, you will have started an entirely *new* cycle; one of walking in, enjoying and manifesting the luscious fruit that comes from being *rooted in* and *walking in,* the incredible, unconditional love of God!

>> See <u>Reflection #9</u> and the <u>Final Reflection</u> in the back of the book. <<

Reflections

>> **Reflection #1** <<

Can you think of a time when you felt the pangs of rejection? Perhaps you are experiencing those now.

Write your experience(s), thought(s) and feeling(s) here.

____

____

____

____

____

____

____

____

____

____

____

____

____

>> **Reflection #2** <<

Now that you know the origin of rejection (that it began in the garden as a result of disobedience, self and sin), how does that help you to understand the beginning of detrimental fruit? Write your thoughts.

____

____

____

____

____

____

____

____

____

____

____

____

>> **Reflection #3** <<

<u>The Root of Rejection Yields the Fruit of Rejection</u>
defensiveness
hardness
anger
rebellion
disrespect
anxiety
depression
insecurities
competition
jealousy
perfectionism
meanness
wishing ill will of others
seeking vengeance
bitterness
inconsistency
impatience
loneliness
fear of what someone thinks about you

Review the table on the previous page. Which of the detrimental fruit do you see in your own life? How did/does this affect your relationship with others? How did/does this affect your relationship with God? Write your thoughts.

>> **Reflection #4** <<

On the following page, the table from chapter 5 is reprinted with the right column left blank. As you allow God to change and heal you, you will see the negative fruit change to positive fruit. Write the resulting positive fruit in the right column of the table. (You may use the words provided in the right column of the table in Chapter 5, or record your own words.) This is a great way to mark your progress!

The Root of Rejection Yields the Fruit of Rejection	The Root of God's Unconditional Love Yields the Fruit of God's Unconditional Love
defensiveness	
hardness	
anger	
rebellion	
disrespect	
anxiety	
depression	
insecurities	
competition	
jealousy	
perfectionism	
meanness	
wishing ill will of others	
seeking vengeance	
bitterness	
inconsistency	
impatience	
loneliness	
fear of what someone thinks about you	

What changes do you see taking place as you take the needed time to get into God's Presence and reflect on Him? Ask Him to show you ways of *how* He loves you! It might be something so beautifully simple as when you needed a smile from someone and that person gave it, or maybe you received a text message or an unexpected blessing from someone. Think about those things! Don't just let them pass you by; **look for them**. God will begin to show you all of the many ways and blessings that He has for you! Write your thoughts and discoveries.

____

____

____

____

____

____

____

____

____

____

>> **Reflection #6** <<

What lies have you believed? Write some of those lies down and, alongside the lie, write the truth from the Bible to knock out that lie!

>> **Reflection #7** <<

Write Galatians 6:4 and 2 Corinthians 10:12. Also, write the truths these Scriptures are saying to YOU.

Galatians 6:4

____

____

____

____

____

____

____

What is Galatians 6:4 saying to you?

____

____

____

____

____

____

____

2 Corinthians 10:12

____

____

____

____

____

____

What is 2 Corinthians 10:12 saying to you?

____

____

____

____

____

____

Have you ever had to *encourage yourself in the Lord?* What did you do to accomplish this? What are some *good* things that you have seen the Lord *already do* for you that would help encourage you? Write your thoughts.

61

>> **Reflection #8** <<

After you have prayed the prayer asking God to help you forgive someone, a group of people, or an event, in what way(s) are you beginning to feel the relief of giving it to God and experiencing the freedom of forgiveness? Write your thoughts.

____

____

____

____

____

____

____

____

____

____

____

____

Are there people from whom *you* need to ask their forgiveness? Write your thoughts.

>> **Reflection #9** <<

Write Jeremiah 1:5; Jeremiah 29:11 and Ephesians 2:10. Reflect upon what they are saying. Write the strong truths that confirm that God has a special plan just for YOU! He LOVES you!

Jeremiah 1:5

____

____

____

____

____

____

Jeremiah 29:11

____

____

____

____

____

____

Ephesians 2:10

>> **Final Reflection** <<

Review Reflections #2 - #9. How has your journey through this book and learning of the unconditional love of God changed you? Write your thoughts.

____

____

____

____

____

____

____

____

____

____

____

____

____

Re-read what was recorded in Reflection 1. Now, write your *new* thoughts(s) and feeling(s) of that experience.

Are there any additional experiences that you may have new thoughts and feelings about?

____

____

____

____

____

____

____

____

____

____

____

____

____

____

____

____

God Says You Are...

1. Designed with *intentionality*. You were ON PURPOSE!

For You formed my inward parts;
You covered me in my mother's womb.
I will praise You, for I am fearfully and
wonderfully made;
Marvelous are Your works,
And that my soul knows very well.
Your eyes saw my substance, being yet
unformed.
And in Your book they all were written,
The days fashioned for me,
When as yet there were none of them.
How precious also are Your thoughts to me,
O God!
How great is the sum of them!
If I should count them, they would be more in
number than the sand;
When I awake, I am still with You.
Psalm 139: 13, 14, 16-18 (NKJV)

2. Created in the image and likeness of God!

Then God said, "Let Us make man in Our
image, according to Our likeness; ... "
Genesis 1:26 (NKJV)

God created us in His image and that is who He is looking for!

3. In Christ, you Have a New Identity

The *moment* you accept Jesus, you have a whole new identity! The *moment* you accepted Christ, you walked out of Adam and you walked into Christ! In Christ, you are a brand new race. In Him, you are a brand new creation! You have a new nature, a new seed, a new DNA from God!

> *For we are God's masterpiece. He has*
> *created us anew in Christ Jesus, so we can*
> *do the good things he planned for us long*
> *ago*
>
> Ephesians 2:10 (NLT)

The word *created* in Ephesians 2:10 that is the same word used in **Genesis 1:1** where God **created** the heavens and the earth. He used that same *creative power* to fashion your new spirit man! There never has been, nor never will be again, someone like you. You are unique, specifically fashioned by a wondrous God!

4. Chosen

> *just as He chose us in Him before the*
> *foundation of the world, that we should be*
> *holy and without blame before Him in love,*
>
> Ephesians 1:4 (NKJV)

Christ "chose us" out of the world to *bring us into Himself*!

> *But you are a **chosen** generation, a royal priesthood, a holy nation, His own special people, that you may proclaim the praises of Him who called you out of darkness into His marvelous light; who once were not a people but are now the people of God, who had not obtained mercy but now have obtained mercy.*
>
> 1 Peter 2:9-10 (NKJV)
> [Bold added for emphasis]

> *Coming to Him as to a living stone, rejected indeed by men, but chosen by God and precious…*
>
> 1 Peter 2:4 (NKJV)

He was *chosen* by God; *that* is what made Him precious; *that* is what determined His worth.

5. Adopted

> *having predestined us to adoption as sons by Jesus Christ to Himself, according to the good pleasure of His will,*
>
> Ephesians 1:5 (NKJV)

Adoption means leaving one family and joining another, leaving behind all that was involved in the first family and **assuming the name, identity,** resources, and history of another. We have left the family of Adam and when we are in Christ, we belong to a new family, the family of Jesus Christ. We've been transferred into a new family, and we have received a new identity.

6. Graciously favored

> *to the praise of the glory of His grace, by*
> *which He made us accepted in the Beloved.*
>
> Ephesians 1:6 (NKJV)

7. Redeemed

> *In Him we have redemption [that is, our*
> *deliverance and salvation] through His*
> *blood, [which paid the penalty for our sin*
> *and resulted in] the forgiveness and complete*
> *pardon of our sin, in accordance with the*
> *riches of His grace*
>
> Ephesians 1:7 (AMP)

Redeemed means to be free from captivity; free from sin and the penalty of sin!

8. Forgiven

*In Him we have redemption [that is, our
deliverance and salvation] through His
blood, [which paid the penalty for our sin
and resulted in] the forgiveness and complete
pardon of our sin, in accordance with the
riches of His grace*
Ephesians 1:7 (AMP)

9. Delivered

*For he has rescued us from the kingdom of
darkness and transferred us into the
Kingdom of his dear Son, who purchased our
freedom and forgave our sins.*
Colossians 1:13-14 (NLT)

10. An heir and a joint heir of Jesus Christ

*The Spirit Himself testifies and confirms
together with our spirit [assuring us] that we
[believers] are children of God. And if [we
are His] children, [then we are His] heirs
also: heirs of God and fellow heirs with
Christ [sharing His spiritual blessing and
inheritance], if indeed we share in His
suffering so that we may also share in His
glory.*
Romans 8:16-17 (AMP)

11. Secure-Sealed by the Holy Spirit

*In Him you also trusted, after you heard the
word of truth, the gospel of your salvation; in
whom also, having believed,* **you were sealed
with the Holy Spirit of promise,**
Ephesians 1:13 (NKJV)
[Bold added for emphasis]

Sealing means that God owns us and will keep us.
We are utterly secure in Christ.

*nor height, nor depth, nor any other created
thing, will be able to separate us from the
[unlimited] love of God, which is in Christ
Jesus our Lord.*
Romans 8:39 (AMP)

*My Father, who has given them to Me, is
greater than all; and no one is able to snatch
them out of My Father's hand.*
John 10:29 (NKJV)

*Let your character [your moral essence, your
inner nature] be free from the love of money
[shun greed—be financially ethical], being
content with what you have; for He has said,
"I will never [under any circumstances]
desert you [nor give you up nor leave you
without support, nor will I in any degree
leave you helpless], nor will I forsake or let*

*you down or relax My hold on you [assuredly
not]!"*

Hebrews 13:5 (AMP)

12. You Have God's Spirit

*Now hope does not disappoint, because the
love of God has been poured out in our
hearts by the Holy Spirit **who was given to
us.***

Romans 5:5 (NKJV)
[Bold added for emphasis]

*the Spirit of truth, whom the world cannot
receive, because it neither sees Him nor
knows Him; but you know Him, **for He
dwells with you and will be in you.***

John 14:17 (NKJV)
[Bold added for emphasis]

*Nevertheless I tell you the truth. It is to your
advantage that I go away; for if I do not go
away, the Helper will not come to you; but if
I depart, **I will send Him to you.***

John 16:7 (NKJV)
[Bold added for emphasis]

*However, when He, the Spirit of truth, has come, **He will guide you into all truth;** for He will not speak on His own authority, but whatever He hears He will speak; and He will tell you things to come.*
John 16:13 (NKJV)
[Bold added for emphasis]

*But you shall **receive power** when the Holy Spirit has come upon you; and you shall be witnesses to Me in Jerusalem, and in all Judea and Samaria, and to the end of the earth.*
Acts 1:8 (NKJV)
[Bold added for emphasis]

I say then: Walk in the Spirit, and you shall not fulfill the lust of the flesh.
Galatians 5:16 (NKJV)

13. Victorious

But thanks be to God, who gives us the victory through our Lord Jesus Christ.
1 Corinthians 15:57 (NKJV)

14. A citizen of heaven

*For our citizenship is in heaven, from which
we also eagerly wait for the Savior, the Lord
Jesus Christ,*
Philippians 3:20 (NKJV)

15. God's Possession

*What agreement is there between the temple
of God and idols? For we are the temple of
the living God; just as God said:
"I will dwell among them and walk among
them;
And I will be their God, and they shall be My
people.*
2 Corinthians 6:16 (AMP)

16. A Royal Priest

*But you are a chosen generation, a royal
priesthood, a holy nation, His own special
people...*
1 Peter 2:9 (NKJV)

You have immediate access to God—you don't need another human priest as a mediator. God Himself provided the one Mediator between God and man, Jesus Christ.

17. An ambassador for Christ

Now then, we are ambassadors for Christ...
2 Corinthians 5:20 (NKJV)

18. You have a glorious future

For I consider that the sufferings of this present time are not worthy to be compared with the glory which shall be revealed in us.
Romans 8:18 (NKJV)

Salvation Through Christ

Jesus answered and said to him, "Most assuredly, I say to you, unless one is born again, he cannot see the kingdom of God." Nicodemus said to Him, "How can a man be born when he is old? Can he enter a second time into his mother's womb and be born?" Jesus answered, "Most assuredly, I say to you, unless one is born of water and the Spirit, he cannot enter the kingdom of God. That which is born of the flesh is flesh, and that which is born of the Spirit is spirit.
John 3:3-6 (NKJV)

The Bible says, "For all have sinned and come short of the glory of God." (Romans 3:23, NKJV) When Adam sinned in the Garden, sin came into the world. This separated man from God. But Christ Jesus came to undo that separation - to reunite man, once again, to God Almighty. Jesus did this by dying on the cross for our sins and rising again from the grave. He made the way possible for us to once again be united with our Heavenly Father and live forever with Him in heaven.

Salvation is a free gift from God. We receive this free gift when we believe and trust in the Lord Jesus Christ. We must trust Jesus Christ and ask Him into our hearts to save us from eternal destruction - to bridge that separation due to sin, to reunite us with the Father…to be our Lord and our Savior.

*...if you confess with your mouth the Lord
Jesus and believe in your heart that God has
raised Him from the dead, you will be saved.
For with
the heart one believes unto righteousness,
and with the mouth confession is made unto
salvation.*
Romans 10:9-10 (NKJV)

*"And this is the will of Him who sent Me,
that everyone who sees the Son and believes
in Him may have everlasting life; and I will
raise him up at the last day."*
John 6:40 (NKJV)

*"He who believes in the Son has eternal life;
but he who does not obey the Son shall not
see life, but the wrath of God abides on
him."*
John 3:36 (NKJV)

The Bible says that there is salvation in no other...

*Jesus said to him, "I am the way, the truth,
and the life. No one comes to the Father
except through Me.*
John 14:6 (NKJV)

Nor is there salvation in any other, for there is no other name under heaven given among men by which we must be saved.

Acts 4:12 (NKJV)

Salvation Prayer

Lord Jesus, I know that I am a sinner. I recognize my need for a Savior. I am so sorry for my sins. I believe that You died on the cross for me and that You rose from the dead. I ask You to forgive me now. Please come into my heart and be my Lord and Savior. I want to know You! I love You! Thank You for saving me.

Congratulations - Welcome to the family of God. If you have any questions or if we can be of any assistance, please contact us at:

Anna Donahue Ministries
PO Box 644
Destrehan, La. 70047

administries@cox.net

(504) 451-4804

ANNADONAHUEMINISTRIES.COM

Sources

1,2. McGee, Robert. *The Search for Significance.* Nashville: Word Publishing, 1998. Print.

3. Krulwich, R. (2012, September 17). *Which Is Greater, The Number Of Sand Grains On Earth Or Stars In The Sky?*. Retrieved from https://www.wbur.org/npr/161096233/which-is-greater-the-number-of-sand-grains-on-earth-or-stars-in-the-sky

4. Renner, Rick. *Sparkling Gems from the Greek.* Tulsa: Rick Renner Ministries, 2003. Print.

5. *Kingdom Dynamics-Spirit-filled Life Bible.* General Editor Jack W. Hayford, Thomas Nelson Publishers, 1991

Other Books by Anna Donahue

Power Love and a Sound Mind
**Freedom from Anxiety, Fear and other Destructive
Thinking!**

*For God has not given us a spirit of fear, but
of power and of love and of a sound mind.*
2 Timothy 1:7

Freedom for anxiety, fear and other destructive
thinking is God's goal for each and every one of us. This
book is a 'hands on' tool of dynamite the will help you to
recognize where the anxiety and fear are coming from, to
learn of the provision that God had made available to us to

eradicate that anxiety and fear, and to walk in that freedom and victory forever.

Determined

If God is for us....

Romans 8:31

(mini-book)

Do you have areas in your life that you would love to see change? Or maybe you have been believing for something to take place in your life and it just hasn't happened yet! God is so amazing! Allow Him to fuel you with His determination to go far and above what you could have ever imagined! All of heaven is waiting to back you! You've got the goods! Be determined to do it!

Fresh Start
God has a new beginning - waiting just for you

You can't put 'new' wine into 'old' wineskins
Luke 5:37-38

(mini-book)

Do you sense something new is on the horizon for you? It is! But, you must be flexible and yield to its arrival! Don't let it spill out and be wasted through stubbornness and inflexibility. No matter what you have been through or where you are right now, God has a 'fresh' encounter waiting just for you!

www.ingramcontent.com/pod-product-compliance
Lightning Source LLC
Chambersburg PA
CBHW031323060726
47590CB00003B/1315